big & SMALL

Original Korean text by In-sook Kim

Illustrations by Do-gyeong Kim

Korean edition © Aram Publishing

This English edition published by big & SMALL in 2016

by arrangement with Aram Publishing

English text edited by Joy Cowley

English edition © big & SMALL 2016

ISBN: 978-1-925234-25-1

Printed in Korea

Running an Errand

Written by In-sook Kim
Illustrated by Do-gyeong Kim
Edited by Joy Cowley

Mum said to Luke,
"Will you go to the shop
and buy an egg for my bread?"

Luke said, "Sure, Mum!"
and away he ran.

Luke said to Mrs Cat,
"I'm running an errand
to buy an egg for Mum."

"Oh, that's good," said Mrs Cat.
"Will you get two eggs for me?
I want to make a fluffy omelet."

Luke hummed a little song.
"I'm running an errand to buy eggs.
I'm going to buy three eggs
because one plus two is three."

Granny Goat called to him
"Luke, please get me an egg too.
I need an egg for a sandwich."

One plus two equals three.
1 + 2 = 3

Luke ran towards the shop.
"I'm going to buy four eggs,
because three plus one is four."

Mr Bear said, "I need an egg too.
Will you please get one for me?"

Three plus one equals four.
3 + 1 = 4

Luke skipped happily along the road.
"I'm running an errand to buy some eggs.
I'm going to buy five eggs,
because four plus one equals five."

Four plus one equals five.
4 + 1 = 5

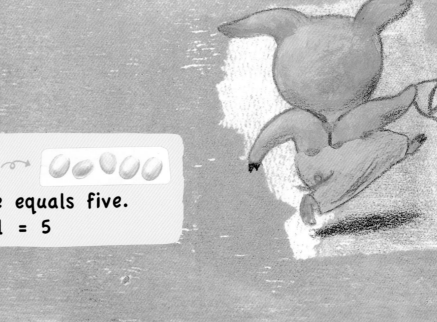

When Luke arrived at the shop,
he saw many customers.
No one spoke to him.

After a long time, Mr Ram said,

"Hi, piglet! What can I do for you?"

"I want eggs," said Luke.

"How many?" asked Mr Ram.

But Luke could not remember how many.

Luke said, "One for Mum
and two for Mrs Cat…"

"Then you need three eggs,"
said Uncle Hippopotamus.

"Then I met Granny Goat and she needed an egg to make a sandwich."

Uncle Crocodile said to Luke, "Then you need four eggs."

"Wait!" said Luke. "I have to buy more.
I met Mr Bear too, and he asked me –"

"Mr Bear would need at least ten eggs,"
said Uncle Giraffe.

"Now, I remember!" shouted Luke.
"Mr Bear also wanted one egg!"

"Did he?" said Uncle Rhinoceros.
"Then you need to buy five eggs,
because four plus one equals five."

"That's it!" said Luke. "One for Mum,
two for Mrs Cat, one for Granny Goat
and one for Mr Bear. That's five!"

Luke ran home, swinging his basket.
"Look at me! I bought these eggs.
I ran an errand all by myself."

Luke is running an errand!

Luke is going to the shop to buy eggs.
How many are needed?

Mum asked for an egg.

Mrs Cat asked for two eggs
Two added to one equals three.

Granny Goat asked for one egg.
One added to three equals four.

Mr Bear asked for one egg.
One added to four equals five.

Math Match!

Draw a line to match the part of the story with the addition sentence.

Mum asked for an egg.
Mrs Cat asked for two eggs.
Two added to one equals three.

$$1 + 3 = 4$$

Granny Goat asked for one egg.
One added to three equals four.

$$1 + 4 = 5$$

Mr Bear asked for one egg.
One added to four equals five.

$$1 + 2 = 3$$

Let's play with addition.

Let's play a game to practise buying things with Mum.
The marbles show the price of each item.

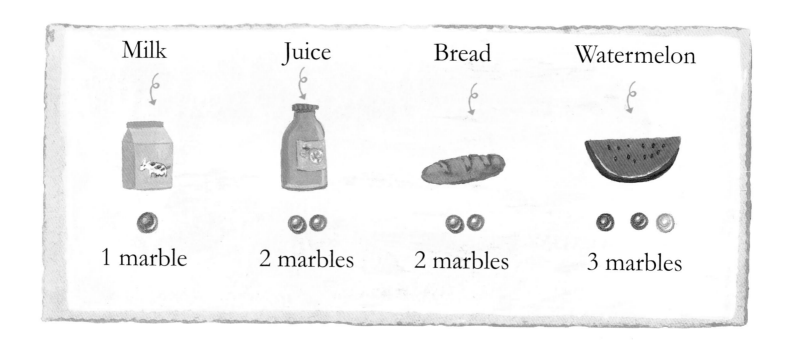

Milk	Juice	Bread	Watermelon
1 marble	2 marbles	2 marbles	3 marbles

If you want to buy a carton of milk and a bottle of juice,
how many marbles do you need?

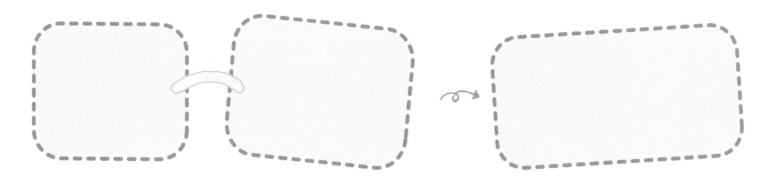

Plant tulips with Mum. Mum plants two tulips, then you plant three. How many tulips are planted in all?

Make a tower with paper cups. If two cups are added to three cups, how many cups will be in the tower?

Cut out pieces of thick paper or use index cards to put between the cups.